My Little Chick

كتكوتى الصغير

English-Arabic

Author : KAMBIZ KAKAVAND
Illustrator : ALI MAFAKHERI

1

Kakavand, Kambiz
My Little Chick
Dual language children's book

Illustrator : Ali Mafakheri

Arabic Translator : Anis-ur-Rehman

ISBN : 81-7650-243-X

Published in India for
STAR BOOKS
55, Warren Street,
London W1T 5NW (UK)
Email : indbooks@spduk.fsnet.co.uk

by
Star Publishers Distributors
New Delhi 110002 (India)

Peacock Series
First Edition : 2006

This book has been published in dual language format
under arrangement with Shabaviz Publishing Co., Iran.

Printed at : Public Printing (Delhi) Service

Daddy bought a pair of beautiful pink shoes
for my little sister Leila.

اشترى أبي لأختي الصغيرة 'ليلىٰ' حذاء

ورديا جميلا .

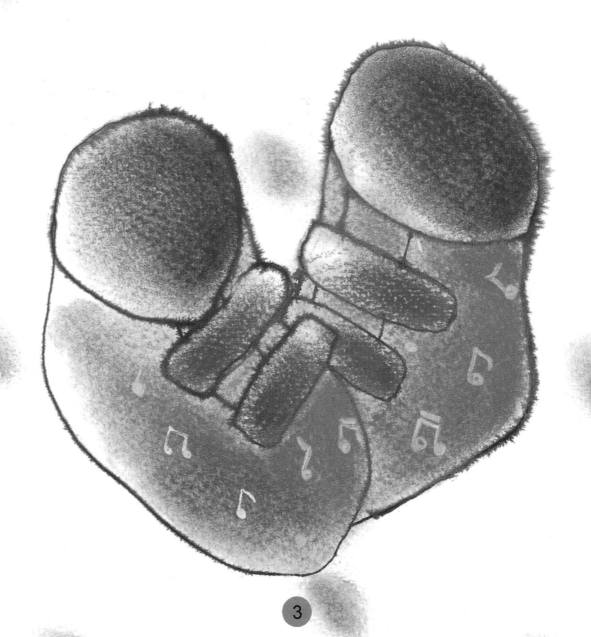

He bought a pair of red shoes for me too.

إنه اشترى لي أيضا حذاء أحمر.

When Leila wore her pink shoes and walked in them,
they made a chirping sound. I loved that sweet sound.

وعندما مشت 'ليلىٰ' بحذائها الوردي أحدث
صوتا غنائيا . وأعجبني ذلك الصوت الجميل .

I said to Daddy, "I also want a pair of chirping shoes."
Mummy immediately replied, "But, dear Sara, you are
a big girl. Only little kids wear chirping shoes."

قلت لأبي : "أنا أيضا أريد حذاء يحدث صوتا غنائيا
مثل هذا."
فقالت الأم بسرعة : "عزيزتي يا سارة إنك قد كبرت
والحذاء الغنائي لا يلبسه إلّا الأطفال الصغار."

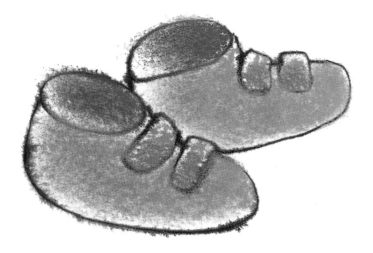

Next morning, Mummy and I went to the market. Mummy bought some fruits and vegetables. As we were returning home, I suddenly heard a chirping sound. I turned back and saw some chicks in a basket in one corner. The chicks were chirping and jumping over each other.

I said to Mummy, "Now that Daddy has not bought chirping shoes for me, please buy me a chirping chick."

ثم في اليوم التالي ذهبت أنا و أمي إلى السوق معا . اشترت الأم شيئا من الخضر والفواكه . فلمّا انصرفنا للرجوع سمعت صوت سقسقة الطيور . فالتفتُّ ورائي و رأيت أن هناك عددا من الكتاكيت موضوعة في سلة . وكانت كلّها تسقسق و تقفز بعضها على بعض .

قلت لأمي : ''بما أن أبي لم يشتر لي حذاء غنائيا فاشتري أنت يا أمي لي كتكوتا واحدا يسقسق .''

I saw that some chicks were white, some were black, some russet and some speckled. I pointed to a nimble russet chick and said, "I want that chick."

إني لاحظت أن من بين الكتاكيت أبيض و أسود و أسمر و أرقط . فأشرتُ إلى كتكوت أسمر و قلت "إني أريد هذا."

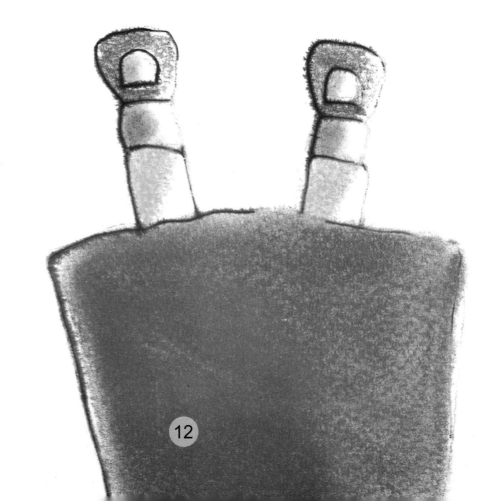

The chicken vendor said, "These are tame chicks. If you feed your chick well and take good care of her, she will grow up soon and lay eggs for you." Mummy bought me the russet chick.

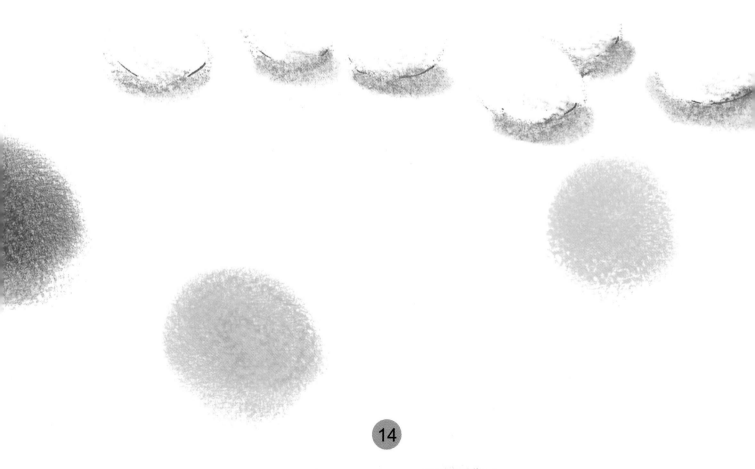

و قال بائع الكتاكيت : "إنها كتاكيت أهلية . إن أطعمت كتكوتك واعتنيت به يكبر بسرعة و ستبيض لك إن كانت دجاجة ." فاشترت لي الأم ذلك الكتكوت الأسمر .

18

Russet Chick could not chirp at all. When I threw seeds in front of her, she would simply eat them quietly. I said to her, "Now say, 'chirp, chirp'. Leila's shoes make a chirping sound. You too must make a chirping sound for me." But Russet Chick did not chirp and remained silent.

ولكن لم يسقسق الكتكوت الأسمر أبداً . إني إذا ما ألقيت الحَب له أكله و هو صامت . قلت له : "سقسق . إن حذاء ' ليلىٰ ' يحدث صوتاً جميلاً فأحدث لي أنت صوتاً جميلاً مثل ذلك ." ولكنه لم يزل صامتاً .

Russet Chick chirped only when I pressed her in my arms. But Mummy did not like it. She would say, "The poor chick will die if you squeeze her like this."

وكان الكتكوت الأسمر يصوّت و يصيح فقط عندما كنت أضغطه بيديّ. ولكن الأم لا تحب ذلك و تقول: "إن الكتكوت المسكين سيموت إن ضغطته هكذا."

One day, Leila's shoes got soaked in the rain and stopped chirping. I no longer felt bad that my chick did not chirp. Now Leila did not have anything better than my pet.

و ذات يوم ابتل حذاء 'ليلىٰ' فى المطر وانقطع صوته الغنائي الجميل . فأصبحتُ الآن لا يسوءني أن لا يسقسق كتكوتى . أمّا 'ليلىٰ' فلم يكن لها الآن شيء أكثر إعجابا من كتكوتى هذا .

Russet Chick was a lovely chick and I loved her. When Mummy cooked rice for us, I took some for the chick too. I dug out worms from our garden and caught flies with the fly-swap for her.

والكتكوت الأسمر كان جميلا حقا وكنت أحبه حبا جما . وكلّما طبخت الأم الأرز أخذتُ منه مقدارا قليلا لكتكوتي . وكنت أحفر أرض بستاننا و أستخرج له الديدان و أقتنص الحشرات والذباب لأكله.

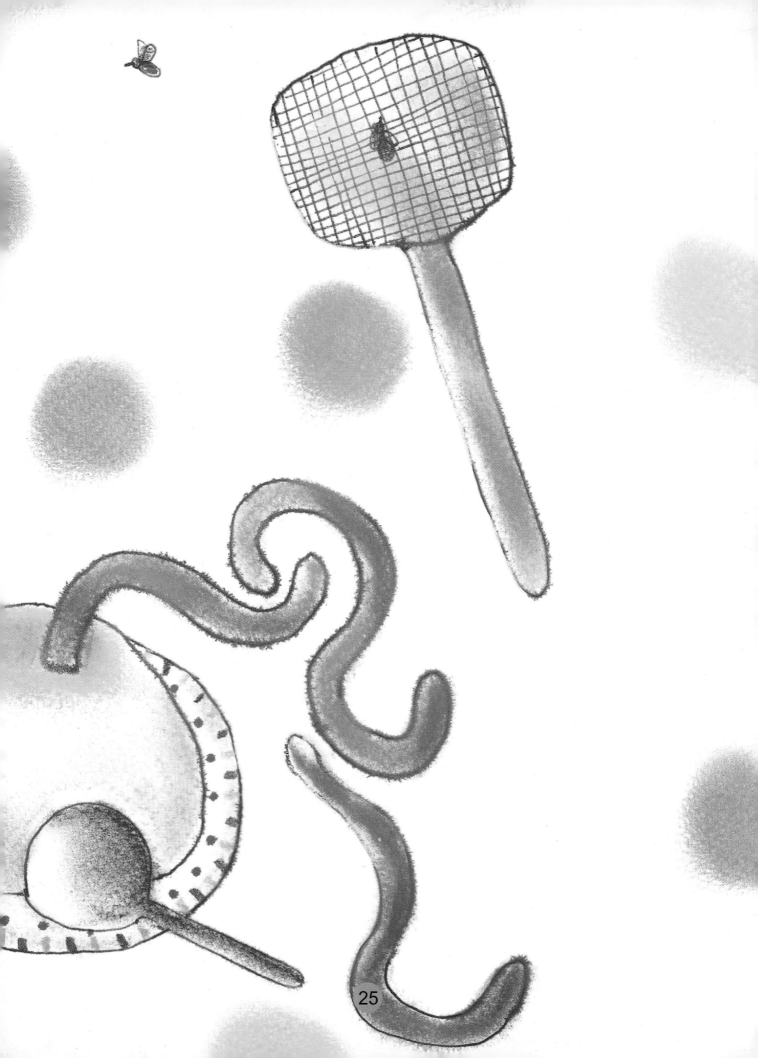

The sparrows would came and sit on the wall of our house and chirp merrily. Russet Chick watched them, but did not utter a sound.
Meanwhile Russet Chick ate and grew big. Plumes grew on her body and a small crown sprung on her head.

وكانت العصافير تأتي و تنزل على جدار دارنا و تسقسق .

والكتكوت الصغير ينظر إليها صامتا ولا يسقسق .

و في تلك الأثناء كبر الكتكوت و قد نبت على جسمه الريش

و نجم على رأسه عرف صغير .

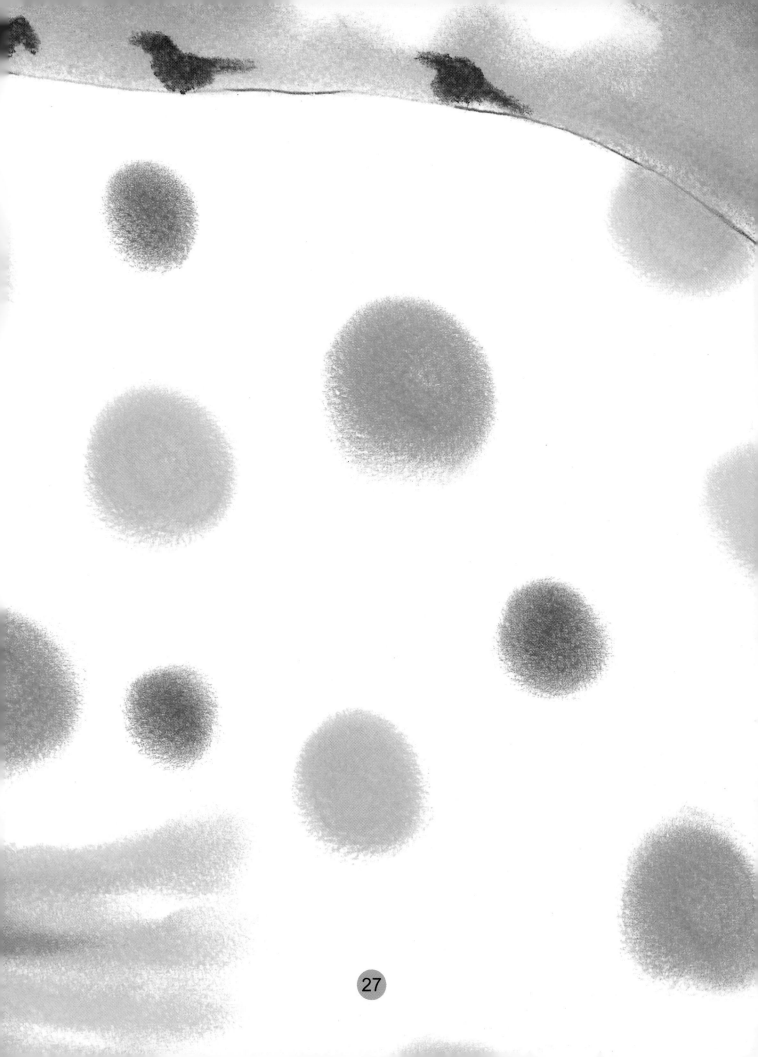

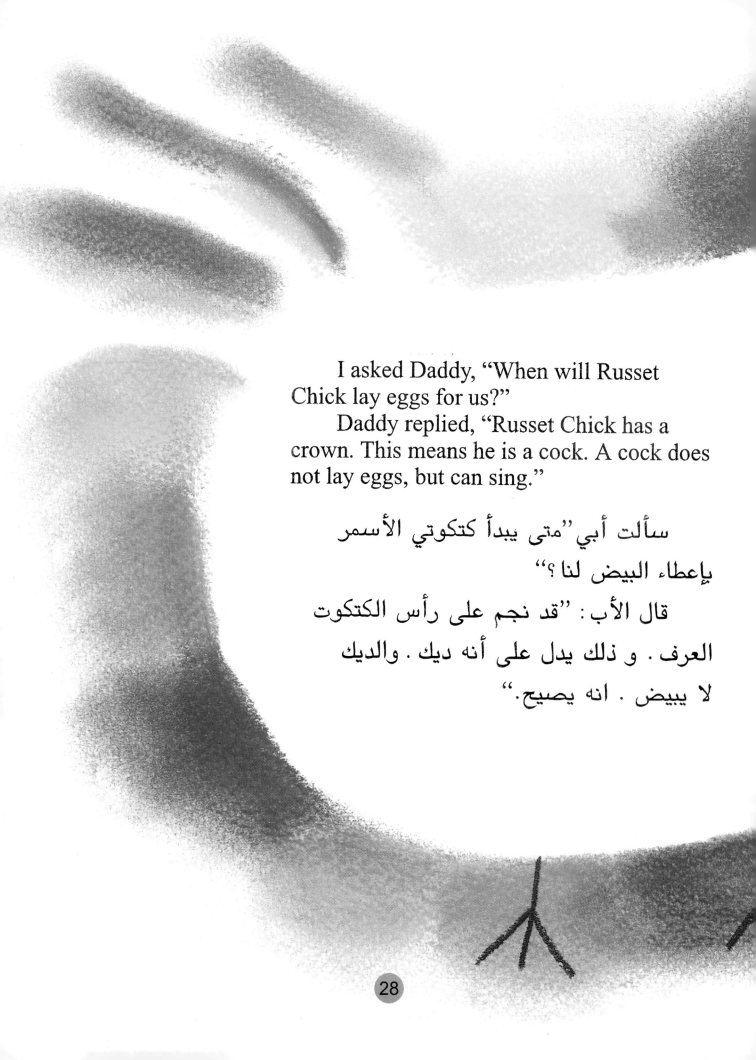

I asked Daddy, "When will Russet Chick lay eggs for us?"

Daddy replied, "Russet Chick has a crown. This means he is a cock. A cock does not lay eggs, but can sing."

سألت أبي "متى يبدأ كتكوتي الأسمر بإعطاء البيض لنا؟"

قال الأب : "قد نجم على رأس الكتكوت العرف . و ذلك يدل على أنه ديك . والديك لا يبيض . انه يصيح."

Several weeks passed. Russet Chick neither chirped, nor lay eggs nor sing. I said to myself, "This chick is useless. He cannot do anything at all. He only eats and eats."

و مرت الأيام أسبوعا بعد أسبوع ، والكتكوت الأسمر لا يصيح ولا يبيض . فقلت "ان هذا الكتكوت بدون فائدة . إنه لا يستطيع شيئا . فهو يأكل و يأكل ولا غير."

One day, as I walked out
with my brother to go to school,
I suddenly heard a song. I looked
around and saw Russet Chick
perched on the wall of our house,
and singing merrily. I was very
happy. My chick who could not
even chirp till now, had grown into
a beautiful cock and was loudly
singing 'Cock-a-doodle doo'.

وفي ذات يوم عندما خرجت من البيت للذهاب إلى المدرسة مع
أخي سمعت صياح الديك فالتفتُّ ورائي و نظرت حولي . فإذا الكتكوت
الأسمر قد صعد على جدار بيتنا وهو يصيح بابتهاج و سرور . ففرحت
بذلك جدا لأن كتكوتي الذي لم يصح ولم يصوّت قبل هذا قد تحول
الآن ديكا رائعاً و يصيح بصوت عال مرتفع : 'كو- كا- كو' .